# Conscience Pricked

AF654280

Dr. Manish Gupta

BlueRose ONE.com
Stories Matter
New Delhi • London

BLUEROSE PUBLISHERS
India | U.K.



For permissions requests or inquiries regarding this publication, please contact:

BLUEROSE PUBLISHERS
www.BlueRoseONE.com
info@bluerosepublishers.com
+91 8882 898 898
+4407342408967

ISBN: 978-93-7310-997-8

Cover design: Aman Sharma
Typesetting: Manisha

First Edition: September 2025

# Preface

My book 'Conscience Pricked' is dedicated to my mother who struggled hard against all odds to educate me. I am also thankful to my wife and children without whose support and encouragement writing this book wouldn't have been possible. I further thank my teachers and all my dear friends who are the tension busters and cause of the smile on my face. I am indebted to my friend Neeraj Kumar who had been very kind and supportive to me in my schooldays.

This book is a collection of ten stories based upon true incidents and experiences of life. Each and every story has a message to convey to its readers over a variety of social evils and practices which are targeted upon by means of a blend of humor and sarcasm. The concluding part of every story will touch your heart and prick your conscience.

**Dr. Manish Gupta.**

# Introduction

'Conscience Pricked' is a collection of ten stories based upon true incidents. Each story has a unique message for the reader.

Snickers of Deprivation is the story of a small school boy, the challenges that he faces due to poverty and lack of resources, and learns to smile when stung with deprivation.

Forfending the Family Pride narrates the story of six children, who collectively fight hunger, without letting their neighbours know that they are without food and forfend their family pride.

Conscience Pricked deals with how self centered human beings are that they overlook the pain and sorrow of others, in their blind race of materialism.

Consecrating a seat in Paradise is sarcasm on how our superstitions lead us into the debt trap.

Amity Lynched is a story that reflects the goodness in human beings, even when they are encircled with hatred. It also suggests a message to promote national integrity.

Phulwa's reunion with smile is the story of how painful and traumatic child labour is when children are exposed to forced separation from their family for earning their livelihood.

Impaired Justice is the story of an unemployed tribal youth who tries to earn his livelihood by digging and carrying sacs of coal to the town but due to his misfortune, falls prey to a corrupt policeman.

The Tribal Vanity is a story regarding enmity between two rival tribal clans that end up due to the bonding of sports between them.

Vermilion Application Hymn via Satellite is a story full of humour and sarcasm on rituals in our society.

Informal Success is the story of a tribal girl Sonamuni who steers her way from being unsuccessful in exams to success in life through informal means. It questions the applicative validity of formal education in its present form.

In a nutshell, all the ten stories of 'Conscience Pricked', pricks your conscience regarding the social evils, superstitions, apathy towards the poverty-stricken human beings and the relevance of our educational system. The concluding part of each and every story will touch your heart and prick your conscience.

**Dr. Manish Gupta**

# Contents

# Snickers of Deprivation

Manu, a student of the primary section, found it difficult to acclimate in a highly reputed English Medium school. Reputation of any educational institution is generally measured in terms of its high-rise buildings, discipline, educational outcomes and the extent to which it can resort to stick to its defined principles. Most of such schools are convents, which run for the charity of mankind, to bring greater glory to God. Charity which is generosity and helpfulness, especially towards the needy or those who are suffering, is actually limited and undermined by philanthropy only for those who belong only to their own religion. Compassion is trimmed to helpfulness towards the needy or suffering, who belong to the same religion, or belief as that of the benefactor. The incorporeal divine Supreme Being ruling over all of us as eternal spirit is perhaps segregated as our God and their God.

Manu's father was an unemployed person; his mother was good at stitching clothes and making beautiful floral patterns on the sari. Her vocation in stitching earned the family a meagre income, which could hardly help them meet the two ends of a family of eight stomachs to be filled. Manu's parents had a sumptuous ancestral home. They were the owners of properties with petty rubric disputes. They had wealth which could not be exploited for the generation of income. They had poverty in the lap of affluence. Veena's friend, Shakuntla, got Manu admitted to the prestigious school with the help of her influential husband, who was a civil engineer and had designed the school building. The school was situated in the outskirts of the town and quite far from their house, so, Shakuntala made an arrangement for Manu's seat on the pedestal of the rickshaw below the seat of the rickshaw's main seat, as the seats were to be occupied by her own children and it was not wide enough to adjust Manu as well. It is an arduous task for a child with paucity of resources to acclimate in a place which is structured for opulence.

Meeting the requirements of the school was an arduous task for Manu and his family. Soon, his uniform lost its lustre, the shoes were torn and worn out and opened its mouth as if they were voicing the child's scarcity. The socks are like the true friends of the poor, they prevent the insult by going inside the shoes, with several holes in it.

The arduous day in school started with the assembly for prayers. In his prayers Manu would plead to God, to have compassion upon him and create some miracle with which he would not be caught and scolded or even got punished by his teachers for his shabby uniform and untidy looks. Once in a blue moon, God would hear his prayers and it would start raining before, or during the prayers and the students would run in a chaos towards their classrooms, saving him from the wrath of the teachers. God's grace came only during the monsoons and for a better part of the year, his prayers went unheard, and Manu would be exposed to the infliction of intense mental and physical agony, straining his fervour for studies.

Manu realised that his teachers could never be wrong because they were the representatives of God as defined in the religious texts and treated his teachers with a stature, which was greater than God. He realised that his white shirt had lost its lustre and had turned pale yellow and it was natural for him to be easily identified amongst sparkling white shirts. He was like a blot on a white sheet of paper. The presence of a student in shabby uniform would not bring a greater glory to God. So he deserved the treatment that he received in school. In his tender age, he had realised that the uniform was more valuable than the living soul inside it.

One whacking day, his parents had nothing to feed him before going to school. His father read the expression on his son's face and consoled him by saying that he would surely bring some food for him during his lunch break. In those days the Government did not have the farsightedness and prudence to distribute freebies among the have not's and stay in power. It would be of no use to Manu, even if the opposite would be the case, as the private schools are outside the purview of Government's welfare schemes.

Manu's hunger would hardly let him concentrate on studies. He was even whipped by his class teacher for not being attentive in the class. The scars on his palm due to whipping seemed like cutting off the lines that were bestowed by God on his palm.

Somehow, half of the school day passed and the bell for the lunch break rang. The day scholars opened their lunch boxes for brunch, the hostellers went to the dining hall for their lunch. The poor tribal students, whose parents had crossed over to the religion of the benefactors, went in a separate line to their own dining hall. Manu headed towards the school's main gate in the hope that his father would have come with some food as he had promised. His father was nowhere to be seen. He peeped out on the lonely road, as far as he could from the closed, main gate. He asked the gatekeeper if someone had come before lunch break and handed over a lunchbox for him. But he got the answer in the negative. Still he had hope against the hope that his father would surely keep his promise, and kept on staring towards the road. Nearly when his hope was about to die, he saw his father approaching from a distant far. His father handed him the lunchbox. He hurriedly took the lunchbox from his father's hand, bid him goodbye, and ran towards the lonely, extreme end of the school boundary. He knew that the contents inside the lunchbox could not be shown to the other school mates, as it would expose him to mockery by his friends.

Manu reached the lonely part of the school premises and opened the lunch box; it contained a thick chapatti smeared with mustard oil and salt. He tried to break the chapatti with his hands, just then, he heard a sound, 'zapp', an eagle had snatched the chapatti from his hands and left three lines of scratch with its claws. Blood oozed out of the scratches, and gave him a sharp burning sensation. The scratches least bothered him, he looked towards the eagle soaring high in the skies with his chapatti, and then settled on the top of the school building to feast upon it. Manu had tears in his eyes, but a smile on his face. He had learnt a lesson, that, if the poor wanted to smile, they should know the art of snatching it from the agony of deprivation. Manu had snickers of deprivation.

# Forfending the Family Pride

Deprivation is a University, which teaches the archaic of survival to its students. Its applicative classes, being the life itself and the challenges in life are the arduous questions that are to be retorted with solidity of character. Very few people have the intrepidity to pass it with distinction.

Sarita was a girl, in her late teens, who had been born in a rich family which was poverty stricken before she could enter her teenage. The family was considered to be one of the most influential and its opulence could be matched by only a few in the town. Prosperity breeds in unity and clashes within the kin opens the door of deprivation.

Sarita's family witnessed both the cases. They had inimitable wealth, when her grandfather and two of his younger brothers lived in solidarity. The eldest Lakhi Chand knew the art of earning money through means of trade. The younger one, Gulab Chand had leadership qualities and harnessed his skill to be a prominent post holder of the party in power. The youngest brother Kesto Chand knew the science of being selfish, and clandestinely amassed money on the exploits of his elder brothers. Things were normal until Lakhi Chand started running into losses in his business, the credit for a larger part of it, went to his youngest brother's clandestine activities. Power follows the footprints of wealth, it comes and goes in the same direction as that of wealth. One's tongue becomes bitter when he encounters deprivation. Sarita's father, who was the eldest son in the clan, hurt the ego of his uncles with his bitter tongue. His uncles made it sure that all his sources of income were completely dried up and made all the possible arrangements, that Suresh would be brought down to his knees, when his incomes would dry up and his needs would drive him in the refuge of his uncles. A rope's twists remain intact even if it gets burnt. Suresh had been brought up like a pampered child and his ego was so big, that he chose to live in deprivation rather than being subdued and go to his uncles' refuge. Clash of egos within the clan led to drying up of sources of income and their wealth became useless due to family disputes.

Sarita, the eldest daughter of Suresh, had witnessed the glorious past of her parents. She too had the blood of her father with tonnes of ego, coupled with self respect. Her father had no other option but to go to Calcutta to work as a clerk in the firm of a relative of his friend. The salary that he received was like cumin in a camel's mouth. It was quite meagre to fulfil the needs of the family, of eight heads, comprising the couple and their six children. The inadequate income could hardly help them meet their two ends. Every now and then, the family members would starve without food. The last week of the month was the most challenging one, with resources being dried up.

In spite of financial crunch and deprivation, the family stood in solidarity, to defend the family pride, as they never let their relatives or neighbours know about their poverty. Just like the smoke, reveals the existence of fire underneath the dried leaves, similarly poverty is revealed, by, the pale faces and the protruding bony structure of the poor. Even if one could judge by the looks that they were poverty stricken, the family members never admitted the fact, because they knew that no one would help them, rather, they would mock at their condition, maybe, not in front of them, but at their back. The family knew that the wealth and riches that had been gone would return one day, but the reputation, once gone, would never return. So, it was better to forfend their family pride, by being pretentious of being well off.

One day, Sarita was given the duty to look after five of her younger siblings. The task was tough because all of them didn't have their dinner due to lack of food at home and it seemed that their fate would continue in the coming day until the parents returned back after making some arrangements from Kolkata. Although Sarita had pretty good leadership qualities, yet, it was hard to lead and take care of five younger brothers and sisters, with empty stomachs, without resources to feed them and make sure that none of them would do something, which would even hint to the neighbours that they were hungry.

Water extinguished their stomach's fire at night, but it ignited with full intensity with the dawn of the next day. It seemed that the whole night all the brothers and sisters were engaged in making plans to fight the battle with hunger the next day in their own way.

With the break of dawn, Sarita went to the nearby garden to collect as many basil leaves as possible, Guddu, went to the nearby hill to pluck Manila tamarind, Abha was busy collecting Aloe Vera leaves, Anil has aiming at the Tamarinds, with sharp edged stones, Honey was busy collecting blue berries and the youngest, Ganesh had gathered honey suckle flowers. In spite of being hungry, none of them had tasted their exploits in solitary. Each and everyone thought that they were the only ones, who were contributing for the whole family and that his, or her effort would earn respect in the eyes of the others and that their effort would be praised.

By seven o'clock in the morning, they had collected enough arsenals to fight against hunger as the six of them had accumulated a nutrition rich breakfast, out of the free gifts of nature. Collectively they had won a battle with their wit and effort but the war had yet to be won. Poverty is the largest university and hunger, the best practical laboratory where miseries are churned to dredge up new ideas.

With the battle of breakfast being won, they again got busy, preparing for the next battle against hunger, during the lunch time. Now they planned to execute their ideas in a united front, under the leadership of Sarita. She instructed her younger brothers Guddu and Anil to demount the brass taps from the iron pipes, which were around ten in number. The taps were useless as water had not flown out of them for five to six years, after; the electricity connection of their house had been cut, due to non-payment of the electricity bills, which were due. The iron pipes would also have been handy, but a better part of it was buried under the cement plaster of the walls through which they ran. Abha and Honey were instructed to collect the dried coal dust balls and cow dung cakes. She herself decided to open the abandoned room and collect used copies, old newspapers, cardboards etc. All of these were to be sold to the scrap dealer Ashokwa, and the proceeds of the sale would be used to buy rice and potatoes, to be cooked in an earthen oven. She instructed her youngest brother aged five to stay in the kitchen and plaster the earthen oven with a paste of mud and water. This task was rendered to him with the dual purpose of keeping him indoors and secondly, it would give her worry free time to think, plan and execute her ideas. Ganesh, in his tender age of five understood, that the best favour that he could do to his family, was to stay safe, indoors and give his elders, a frazzle free time.

The children had meticulously put their plans into action, which fetched them twenty rupees, which was enough to buy coarse rice and potatoes in those early eighties. Sarita handed over the money to her younger brothers to fetch rice and potatoes from the market and in the mean while, instructed her younger sisters to light a fire, in the earthen oven, with the help of, cow dung cakes and the balls of coal dust.

Fortune favours the brave, but rarely the poor and the deprived ones. As her younger brothers were about to depart to buy rice and potatoes, the washer woman entered the house and in a loud and complaining voice demanded the money which had been due on their parents for six months. After the death of their grandmother, the priest and the barber had helped their parents in reserving the seat in heaven for their grandmother by performing certain rituals. The priest and the barber were somehow paid for their favour. It is also customary that all the bed sheets, pillow covers, and each and every clothes and garments of all the family members be washed, by a washer man, to rid them, from the shadow of the departed soul. In a nutshell, the rituals that are performed, after the death of a family member, takes care of, the incomes of, all the professions and trades of the society, except, the family of the bereaved. The entire process of the reservation of seats in heaven for the deceased is quite complex, lengthy and expensive.

The washer woman was in no mood to return without the dues being cleared, because she had a glimpse of money, in the hands of the children. Sarita tried her best, to make her agree upon giving them some more time, or even, taking half of the money that they had. But the cunning washer woman sensed that it was the best opportunity, to take as much money as possible. So, she started shouting, even more loudly and hurling curses on their parents. Until now, Sarita had been using very sweet words to manage her, but the curses being hurled upon her parents were intolerable to her, more so ever, by a woman of lewd associate, and in a voice that could be overheard by the neighbours. Sarita immediately took the money from her brother's hand and handed it over to the lady, simultaneously kicking her out of the door and defending her family pride.

The children realised that they had lost the war against hunger, as they had no resources left, to defend themselves. Asking for help from neighbours was not and never an option. The fire in the earthen oven had been lit, so was the fire of hunger, in their stomachs. Like good soldiers, Sarita and her brothers and sisters, accepted fate, with grace. The whole day she kept her siblings engaged in one game or the other, but soon the younger ones got fed up with the game and lost interest in it, the reason being hunger. Sarita kept on switching over to as many games as she knew. She even invented some games. She wanted to cry, but controlled her emotions, as it would further deteriorate the condition.

Somehow, the sun had set; the children went to bed early, after drinking lots of water. All the six of them lay on the same bed, with their hands entangled upon each other. Sarita tried to help them fall asleep, by singing songs and telling fairy tales, but the songs and the stories were few and the night, longer than ever.

# Conscience Pricked

Some incidents in our life prick the core of our heart and keep on quivering our consciousness. What is our contribution to humanity as human beings? The answer has to be given collectively, by humanity as a whole. Certain incidents in life prick our conscience and impose a question mark on our approach towards humanity which is compendious with apathy towards fellow human beings.

On the way towards my school, there was a four-way road crossing. On the footpath leading towards the crossing, in my busy schedule, I used to come across an ugly, half-naked, ill-fed, thin and stinky lady, who sat there begging in her tent made up of different sized loose brick walls parallel to each other, which ended up with the wall of a tall building on one end and the other end opening towards the footpath side. Though I consider myself to be in the lot of have-nots, yet I disliked her presence on the roadside as if she was a dirty blot in this shining India. I, too, occasionally threw a few coins before her like the other passers to show my hollow sympathy towards her.

Days passed with least changes in her life, but remarkably her lower abdomen was swelling day by day. It protruded out of her bony structure indicating that perhaps, she was expected. Her condition showed how unsafe females are in spite of being stinky, half-mad beggars. Being female is enough to fall prey to such male wolves who keep hunting for a lonely female.

One day, since I was getting late for my school, I was almost running to catch my bus, towards the road crossing, I saw her crying in excruciating pain, lying on the ground, moving her legs too and fro in the dust. People were passing by her and as tokens of sympathy, threw coins beside her as if they were painkillers. Beside her was a half-bitten bread, showing that there were some bigger donors as well. People realized that she needed medical help, which was time consuming and they expected somebody else to do the time riveting work. Their conscience told them to address the call of the distressed lady, but they suppressed it owing to their busy schedule and subdued their scruple by throwing coins towards her, in spite of knowing that the shrouds do not have pockets.

I found myself helpless, it was her delivery time and I knew nothing regarding first aid in such a condition. So, I ran to a nearby government hospital. As usual, the hospital was overcrowded. I somehow managed to reach the doctor's chamber and told him to do something for the lady in distress. The doctor looked towards me and got busy writing the prescription. I kept waiting for his response for another five minutes but he seemed to be unresponsive. I once again insisted that he should make some arrangement to help that lady or at least send an ambulance. This time he looked at me sarcastically and with a cruel smile, he asked me, "What is the matter? Humanity has arisen like a tide in your heart for that lady, hope you are not responsible for her condition?" His expression and words, both infuriated me. Though I was a Gandhian by thought, still at that moment I felt like giving him a good dressing and even operating him. Somehow I controlled my emotions and turned back. An old man who was waiting for his turn to see the doctor, overheard our conversation, said, "why are you worried about her, there are many like her, numbering in thousands, the Government least cares for them, why should you? Leave her to her fate, if she has to live, she will live and if God wishes so, she will die, what can you do?"

The flow of blood in my adrenalin was now at its peak and I burst on him saying, "You old fellow, why have you come to the hospital, if God has to decide for your life and death?" I thought it was better to leave that place as soon as possible before I would get involved in a brawl.

I went back to the place where the lady dwelt, by the time I reached there, she lay dead with her lower abdomen soaked in blood and dust. A few Margosa tree leaves had fallen from the tree on her body. Perhaps even Mother Nature was trying her best to cover the painful nudity of our insouciance towards human beings with the help of those leaves. There were many coins beside her; today she was getting record alms even if she was not alive to beg. Some poor street children gathered around her corpse, with their eyes stuck on the coins. A beggar collected the coins and purchased a shroud with half of the amount collected, to cover the corpse and kept the other half for himself.

After sometime, an ambulance came to the spot and two men dressed in white, put her dead body on a stretcher and filled it in the ambulance. I went to them and asked, "Why have you come now, when you least cared for her, when she was alive?" One of them replied, "We will take the dead body to the medical college, where the medical students will do their practical on this dead body, to become future doctors". I was stunned and speechless when I heard those words. As soon as the ambulance departed, the beggar cleaned the stains of the blood of the deceased and occupied the place as; it had a precise location for begging.

I walked back, towards my house, with an aggrieved, heavy heart, full of frustration, anguish and bitterness towards the hollowness of the human beings. I kept questioning myself, "Are we human beings? , If so, why are we? Animals kill other animals and eat their dead body for survival. But we claim to be human beings. How can we use the living and dead as per our requirements? Has science and materialism still kept us as human beings? Or they have transformed us into human resources with all the types of human emotions being suppressed?"

We are so selfish and self-centered that we care the least for the pain and agony of others. Before doing anything, we weigh the action in a weighing machine of our brain and when we feel we're going to gain by our action, we move forward with that deed.

A beggar who was alive was of least value to the doctor. When he knew that soon she was about to die, he immediately calculated in his mind, how to make the best use of the dead body. After practical, the carcasses would either be dumped in a nearby river or thrown in a lonely place for the scavengers to feed upon them. Burying or burning the dead would again be costly or uneconomical for them.

The incident pricked my conscience, but most of the so-called successful people hardly thought about it. The incident proved that we human beings are ready to roast our bread on the funeral pyre of others. Why is such a small and common incident pricking me? An emotional fool like me will have no money in the pocket with conscience pricking in his heart. The so-called successful people are smart enough to have conquered their emotions, they concentrate upon utilizing their time to amass as much wealth as possible and then donate ' money' as charity.

# Consecrating a seat in Paradise

The love and affection for our near and dear ones burgeon in several folds, when they depart from this world. We suddenly initiate a thought process of his/her virtues and hunt for memories, which support the cause of glorifying the deceased, even if such instances are rare or even non-existent.

The Psychology behind it is that, we will no longer be able to see the departed ones. The feeling of being separated from our dear ones blunts our logical intellection and we readily do whatever is possible from our end, to make the eternal journey of the departed soul, comfortable and full of tranquillity. The aftermath of life is unknown; our knowledge in this field is dark so it is full of predictions, assumptions and illogical reasoning.

Exploitation in the garb of superstitions and complex religious rituals, thrive on the grave of rational thinking. Deductive reasoning gets buried, when our emotions are high. Under these circumstances, the flag bearers of religion propound principles and theories to create a strong aura of systems, beliefs and customs, which are held by the theist, with much ardour and faith.

The death of our father broke us, both psychologically and financially. The modest income of the sole bread earner of our family could hardly save money, for such an unforeseen eventuality. A meticulous family budget is planned when there is any possibility of resources to be saved for the future. All the reasoning and planning evaporate when exposed to the desert of scarcity. Penny-pinching by my mother, helped us, with a meagre saving, which soon evaporated, when my father fell ill, of reasons unknown.

The cost of multifarious tests to diagnose the disease could hardly be met with the proceeds of my mother's savings. So, we had to resort to borrowing money from the money lender as an advance against the ancestral agricultural plot of land. Land is considered to be our mother, and in times of penury, it is the mother, who responds to our call first and foremost. With the detection of lung cancer, the land had to be sold, in order to save my father. It is rightly said that our fates are pre determined by God, so it is wise not to argue over it. My father initially showed signs of recovery, but his life ended with the end of the money resources at our disposal.

It is quite well known that doctors have to study hard for several years to get their prized MBBS degree. But their knowledge is serviceable to the patients, till the patients have money. Money is the oxygen, which helps the patients breathe.

When the corpse of our father was handed over to us, we all burst into tears. Half of our sorrow were for the demise of our loving father and the other half of our sorrow, were regarding how we would further meet the huge expenses of his funeral rites and rituals, that would help us, in consecrating a seat, for our father's departed soul in the paradise, and also ensure a peaceful, comfortable and safe journey, to the heavenly abode.

Our uncle who had never helped us, in any of our needs, not even, during my father's illness, gave my mother five thousand rupees, for carrying out the funeral rites. It is hard for me to judge whether his change of mind was driven by the sorrow, due to the demise of his elder brother, whom he would never see again or, the contentment that he would never have to see his brother again. The justifications to my doubt over my uncle's intentions were drawn from our past experiences. Whatever the case might be, his intentions were of no relevance for us, what was relevant was the money that he had donated to us.

Lions are the apex predators because of their mastery over the knowledge of the hunting ground, its ability to sense the weakness and frail body parts of its prey, coupled by the brute strength. The jackals lack most of these hunting skills, but are cunning enough to pursue the lion, out of the greed, of feasting over the left over carcasses of the hunted prey. Somewhat similar is the mindset of some people who keep on hunting for their prey, when people are psychologically broken they exploit their sentiments and make them emotional fools by means of complex rituals and practices which have no logical base and are irrelevant. Most of the bad loans are taken for these rituals and extravagance when it comes to offerings in terms of money and material for conducting the complex rituals during the birth, marriage or death of the people.

If one has to live in the society, with his head held high and without being mocked at, one has to shun logical reasoning and blindly follow the practices and rituals which were being performed by their ancestors, since times immemorial, irrespective of, whether, they are having the resources to back those expenses, or not.

Like good believers of our faith, we had no other option, but to ensure that our deceased father reached his heavenly abode. For this specific purpose, we have specialists, who are supposed to be born, out of the head of the God Brahma who is supposed to be the creator of this universe, and accordingly, they are seated, at the top of, the social hierarchy in the social division of labour. The mighty ruling class is believed to be born out of the arms and chest of the Supreme Being, known as the Brahma. The business classes and the people, who are further down the social occupational hierarchy, are believed to be born out of the stomach and lower waist part of the Supreme Being's body, respectively. This is the first example of 'reservation' to be known to mankind but never being talked of. Our politicians have perhaps derived the concept of reservation the merits and demerits of which is much debated today.

So, it is natural, that those born out of the head part of the supreme God, will have proximity with God, and he will have an access to God's living abode, the heaven. Since they know the route to paradise, they are in an impressive position to guide the departed soul en route to paradise. Every journey has a cost and there are some essentials, which are to be carried in a journey to avoid hardships. Accordingly, the rituals are performed and donations are being given to the priests, in the pretext of avoiding hardships of the departed soul en route to heaven. We too had to hire some experienced guides, who would ensure our father's journey to paradise by chanting hymns and performing complex rituals from the earth.

My deceased father's soul's journey to paradise initiated with the burning of his body in the cremation ground, which would free his soul from the earthly body in which it was trapped. The fire for the funeral pyre had to be lit by the person in charge of the cremation ground. He demanded ten thousand rupees, for his exclusive right to light a match stick, to ignite fire on a bundle of hay, which would then be used by my elder brother to light the funeral pyre. After much bargaining and pressure being mounted by the people from our society, who had accompanied us to the cremation ground, the deal was settled for two thousand five hundred rupees. In return for the sum of money, he lit the fire in the bundle of hay and after the dead body had been burnt and its ashes immersed in the river Ganga, he even got all of us, rid of, the shadows of the cremation ground, which otherwise, would be the cause of the bad omen, back home.

We reached home and for ten continuous days a barber accompanied my elder brother to the banks of the river, where, my brother would perform rituals as per the direction of the barber, as he was another expert, whose rituals would provide food to the departed soul in the journey towards the heaven, the iron razor in his hand had the capacity to ward off the evil spirits who might be encountered upon while getting connected to the spirits in these processes.

On the tenth day, came the role of the apex predator and the prey was my elder brother, as he was the doer, or the person, who had performed the funeral rites, being the eldest son. After performing, a series of rituals and a mix of complex prayers and rituals, backed by the hymns in Sanskrit language which were a mix of bombastic words with very difficult pronunciation, being sung in a typical musical tone, backed by the sound of the conch at regular intervals to mark the beginning and the end of the subparts of the rituals.

All of us were convinced that the soul was heading in the right trajectory, towards paradise and had reached the gates of paradise. The gates of heaven would be wide open, after the last ritual.

My brother sat in the praying posture with his hair and moustache, which had been shaved off, the very first day, by the barber. He wore a white dhoti, a collection of long white thread, hanging from his right ear, across his chest and stomach to his waist, a white turban, with finger marks of sandal wood, over his forehead, neck, shoulders and arms. The priest sat in front of him and the barber sat at his back. The final onslaught had begun. The priest chanted a hymn and translated it into our language, saying that, the gates of heaven open, by the virtue of good deeds, done on earth, while being alive. "Your father was supposed to build an inn, has he?" The answer to it was negative. Seeing the nervousness on my brother's face, he said, "there is a way out, you give me an offering of money against it." My brother looked towards the priest with a horrified look, as its cost would run into a million of rupees. The priest was wise and passionate enough to relieve his Yajmaan, and told him, to imagine, that he was building an inn and as a compensation for it, pay some amount of money according to his financial status. With a sense of relief, my brother tried to take out a hundred rupee note from his purse. The priest stopped him and told him to keep adding the sum of money in his mind, as; more expenses were yet to come. Similarly, the priest kept on naming, a long series of goods and services, that, were supposed to be donated by our father, while he was alive, such as constructing ponds, wells, temples, donations of bed and bed sheets, table, chair, eatables, clothing, cows, utensils etc. Our father could have hardly afforded to donate these things in his lifetime, because his meagre salary would hardly permit him to do so. My brother kept on, adding up the fractions of those expenses, as the priest had been kind enough to give him the liberty of deciding the amount for those expenses. My brother thought, that, he was cunning enough to underestimate the cost of all the donations, that, were to be made, but, he had forgotten, that, he had taken birth from Brahma's stomach and that he was of no match, for a clan, which had its origin from Brahma's head.

In spite of the costs being under estimated, it summed up to twenty five thousand Indian rupees. All our relatives emptied their pockets and handed over the small sums of money, to my brother, who would pay the offerings to the priest, yet, it summed up to twenty one thousand. The priest was again, very kind, and with a large heartedness, he settled the score with the collected amount of twenty one thousand and gave a discount of four thousand. After the rituals were over the priest kept ninety percent of the offerings for him and left ten percent of the proceeds for the barber as a reward for the arrangements that he had made for the rituals.

With the end of rituals and the offering of money and several materials, the gates of heaven were presumed to be opened for the soul of our departed father. To further strengthen our father's soul's comfortable stay in Paradise, a party was given, to around five hundred people, comprising our relatives, family members and the people of the society, at the cost of being submerged in debt till neck.

# Amity Lynched

Cordiality between me and Shamir Qureshi was looked upon by our classmates as a nonpareil alliance because both of us belonged to dissimilar faiths. The mentality behind it arose from the incertitude between Hindus and Muslims. The inference was drawn from the atrocities done on the Hindus for hundreds of years because they were considered as infidels by the invaders from the western frontiers of India. Each and every time, whenever, India was invaded by the barbarians, Gujarat was the area which bled the most, as it lay on the route towards the Indian capital. Gujarat had to bear the sting of hatred of the invaders the most. Men were slaughtered, women and children taken as slaves and their properties and places of worship were turned to ashes, and their only sin was that of being an infidel, the believers of other faiths. Those, who could not bear the thousand year onslaught, changed their beliefs during the course of time out of the fear of the sword. In this almost thousand years of continuous trauma the people forgot that those practicing the other faiths were their own kinsfolk and continue to clash with each other on trivial issues.

The city of Ahmadabad saw frequent riots, as if the whole city stood over gunpowder, ready to explode anytime, with the fire of a matchstick. The bond of friendship between the teenagers of different faiths was natural to be looked upon with a mixed reaction of both suspicion and the belief that we were ignorant fools. In my fifteen years of age I had never been a witness to riots, nor did I realise the consequence of being caught up in a riot torn area, because things were different in our hometown.

The news of Babri Mosque being demolished at Ayodhya spread like a wild fire. Its chain of events in different cities across India and its consequences were predicted by the Government and all the schools, colleges and business installations were closed in the fear of some untoward incident.

A school holiday for a teenager is the best time for him to spend with his best friend. The delight of spending the whole day gossiping and laughing surmounted the imperiousness of being trapped in a riot torn area like Lal-Darwaza, in Old Ahmadabad city. Around nine o'clock in the morning, I was passing through the roads in the Lal-Darwaza region. There was an unusual silence on the roads which otherwise would be a crisscross of bustling roads, streets and lanes. Hardly one or two people could be seen here and there with perturbed faces. Some policemen could be seen on each and every cross road. The whole area seemed so strange and unwelcoming that I was confused about the right lane that led to Shamir's house. Very few people were seen on the road and those who were present, had grim faces. I tried to clear my doubt regarding the lane that led to Shamir's house by querying for the right address from a person who seemed to be relatively less tense, but his silence convinced me that I was in the wrong place at the wrong time. Fear crept into me and I thought of returning back to my hostel but soon realised that I had come too far, too deep in the enemy lines, in an area that was hostile towards the people of my faith. Returning back would be fatal for me, the only hope of survival was to reach my friend's house and surrender my fate to friendship. In spite of the fact that the lanes with closed shops looked unfamiliar to me, I somehow reached Shamir's house and knocked the main door as hard as I could. Shamir's mother opened the gate with a panic which was created by the sound of the rapid knocking of the door. When she saw me, her face had the double expressions of cordiality and stupefaction. She realised that a big liability was at her door, and if the neighbours would see me entering her house, it would be improbable for her to save me from the hostile, angry mob. She immediately pulled me inside the house and locked the door from inside. My friend welcomed me with a smile and took me to his room which was on the terrace of his two storied building. His father came and instructed him not to expose me on the terrace without a net cap. I understood that his instructions were to save me by disguising me like a person of his faith.

While we were having our breakfast, Mr. Qureshi got news that a person had been stabbed near 'Lal-Darwaza Mosque', on the road that I had crossed a few minutes back. Curfew was imposed and the people were instructed to stay indoors. My fear of being in an area of inimical people was nullified by the realisation that my hosts were not hostile towards me.

At night we could see some strangers coming with a truck loaded with arms and foodstuffs. The deprived ones were given a small sack of food and arms like swords, petrol bombs, crude bombs etc. At midnight, from the terrace we could see stones, petrol bombs and crude bombs, being hurled in between the rioting factions, with the heterogeneous sounds of shouting, yelling, crying, amongst the sounds of blasting petrol bombs, crude bombs and occasional firing on the main road, the opposite sides of which had settlements of the Hindus and the Muslims. It was a cause of concern for the parents but a thrill for the teenagers like us. The scenes of a live rioting exhilarated us, because it was an ecstasy, to watch a live war like situation. Our immature minds did not even; bother about the pain being inflicted upon the victims of the riots. I stayed at Shamir's house for a couple of days until the curfew was removed and things returned to normalcy. Within these few days the affection of Shamir's parents made me feel like one of their family members. While going back to my hostel, I felt the same torment, like that of, when I would return to my hostel leaving back my family members.

The bond of friendship with Shamir came to a falter, when I had to return to my hometown due to my father's illness. We got busy in our own worlds, after that hiatus. But friendship is like a fire that keeps burning in the hearts of friends even when they are not in touch with each other for several decades. In our case I thought of a reunion with my friend after almost thirty years, since our abrupt separation. Although I did not have Shamir's contact number yet, I somehow located his house. His house no longer seemed lively as it used to be when I was their guest. A strange silence and strangeness engulfed the house. A lady came to the door and said that her husband was not there at home and told me to wait outside the house until he returned from his shop. I tried to convince her that I was like one of her family members by talking about

Mr. and Mrs. Qureshi and our school day bond, but she showed least interest in my words and returned back after closing the door. I waited for my friend in a tea-stall, which was a couple of yards away. While sipping the tea, I remembered our school days of how I would pick up a fight with anybody, only to be rescued by Shamir, as his builds were far better than mine. I thought how happy and surprised my friend would be, when he would see me, and might be infuriated with the lady who welcomed me coldly. The thoughts of our school days were quite mesmerizing. The tea stall owner was quite courteous to me when he learnt that I was Shamir's friend and gave me a seat that faced Shamir's house.

After a couple of hours the tea stall owner waved his hand and shouted 'Shamir Bhai jaan', your friend is looking for you." It attracted my attention as well, and I saw a sturdy man with long beards and a serious face. When I looked quite carefully I realised that he was Shamir whose teenager looks were transformed to what it was today. I ran towards him and hugged him saying 'Shamir, I am Manish', do you remember me?" Soon I realised that my friend did not receive me with the warmth that I expected. He sat with me on another seat facing me, and ordered two cups of tea. While sipping tea he inquired about my whereabouts, and retired into a silence when asked about his well-being.

After some time he bid me farewell and headed towards his house, without inviting me to his dwelling place. His strange behaviour was beyond my understanding.

After Shamir's departure, I asked the tea stall owner whether things were alright with him. He told me that during the last riots Shamir's house was attacked by an angry mob, and put on fire, in which his parents were lynched to death. I realised that the angry mob not only lynched Shamir's parents but also our friendship. It was our amity lynched. I felt very sorry for Shamir and my heart was filled with exasperation. I understood the reason why he did not take me to his house. He didn't want me to know about his sorrows and be filled with grief and guilt that the people of my faith were responsible for the lynching of his parents. I ran towards my friend, hugged him and started crying, seeing tears in my eyes. My friend too started crying. The tear of a friend has the capacity to heal the wounds of another friend. Our friendship which had been torn apart by vicious hatred between two different faiths was pasted once again by the glue of our tears. My friend's abhorrence towards the people of my faith was perhaps washed away with those tears. The opposite parties of the clash might also have some similar or even worse catastrophes.

Man, by nature is good and tries his best to uphold human values, but there are fault lines within the society, which create circumstances that coerce them to have thoughts of dissension. In fact, there has never been a genuine effort to soothe the burning sensation in the hearts of the victims of such tragedies, by the Government or by the Civil Society as a whole. The Government pats its back by witch hunting the perpetrators of riots by punishing them and offering some grants in aid to the victims. The Civil Society remains contended with charities and donations for the victims and sometimes harping upon the blame game on either side. But the fact of the matter is that these steps are not serving the purpose of bringing the clashing sides together, rather they are increasing the rift between the two sides.

A nation never emerges to be a great one with amity being lynched.

# Phulwa's Reunion with Smile

Mr. Sharma, a lower middle class person got good news that soon he was going to become the father of a child. Like any other low-income family, such good news is followed by certain liabilities and a huge bundle of wants that are to be met with quite scarce resources at their disposal. The larger concern was that his wife Mrs. Sharma was advised complete bed rest during her pregnancy period. A housewife, who is generally considered as unemployed, as her activities that are done out of love and affection for her family, yield no income. Her activities are considered to be non-economic, but the magnitude of the duties that are regularly performed by her, is perceived, when she is given a bed rest.

Mr. Sharma in spite of his meager income was forced to look for a maid to do the household work. The maid's monthly charges seemed to be ultra expensive for him. He talked about his problem with his elder sister, who lived in a village called Dholi. Like any other elder sister, she advised him to keep a young girl, as a cheaper substitute to regular house maids. Mr. Sharma hesitated, but his sister convinced him that it would be of dual benefit as the female child in poverty-stricken families are not fed and taken care of well, in spite of the industrious work performed by them in the fields. His sister even arranged for an eleven year old girl Phulwa from her village.

The next day Mr. Sharma was at Phulwa's house, giving some advance money, as salary to Phulwa's mother. Phulwa's mother Karoo was a widow with four children. Her husband had been swept away in the flashflood two years back. After a heavy downpour of monsoon rains the barrage was full of water. The embankments of the barrage were not strong enough, the engineers predicted that its western embankment would soon give up and would flood the city of Muzaffarpur, which was one of the prominent cities and a constituency in the state of Bihar. Flooding of a city would attract media attention and the distress for the city requisite with the rich and influential people, would be politically indecorous for the government, resulting in retributory punishment for the top bureaucratic brass. So, a prompt decision was taken to open the gates of the Gandak river barrage, which resulted in a flash flood in the catchment area of the river, inundating the fields and hundreds of villages. Phulwa's father was one among the scores of agriculture laborers who were swept away in those flash floods, while working in the fields.

Every year floods in Bihar bring sorrow for millions of rural folk, but the calamitous floods are a feasting season for the bureaucratic and political class. The huge amount of grants in the name of 'flood relief', which runs into thousands of millions, most of which go unaudited, is quite well-favored of monkey sharing between the bureaucrats and the politicians. Floods effectuate imperilment for the poor, just before the festive season; on the other hand, it invokes proceeds, for the functionary bureaucrats. It all depends on which side of the flood you are on.

Karoo found it difficult to feed four mouths, with her meager income arising out of doing household work. Regardless of her age, Phulwa, being the eldest child of her mother, was expected to earn some money and shoulder the responsibility of taking care of the family along with her mother. Phulwa was considered as an income earning asset for her mother. When she received money from Mr. Sharma, her love and affection for Phulwa evaporated with the warmth of money and she readily agreed to send Phulwa, to a distant unknown land, surrendering her fate into the hands of an unknown man. When Phulwa came to know of her mother's decision, she looked towards her mother with eyes filled with tears, but she didn't cry, fearing her mother's wrath. Before parting, she hugged all her younger siblings, who couldn't understand what was going on, but sensed some tragedy, seeing tears in Phulwa's eyes. They started crying and caught hold of their sister, as hard as they could. Plulwa looked into her mother's eyes as if, questioning her decision. Her mother responded, by looking towards the other side, she too had her eyes, filled with tears, which she quickly wiped off with the fringe of her sari. Phulwa read her mother's expression and understood that her mother now needed her help in earning bread for the family and that it was not her choice, rather, it was her destituteness which was to be blamed. Phulwa took her younger brothers inside the hut and swiftly came out and locked them inside the hut, before they could understand that they had been tricked by their sister.

Phulwa boarded the train along with Mr. Sharma to head towards Sahibganj, where Mr. Sharma lived. She had a vivacious smiling face; her comely prettiness was overshadowed by her dirty crisscross of long brown entangled hairs, dust on her face and patches of dirt on most parts of her hands, legs and face. Her clothes resembled her body. What poverty could not rob of her was the smile on her face, which was now ripped off due to her separation from her family at a tender age.

The long journey of twelve hours by train was widening the distance between her and her family. The childhood innocence, which could not be robbed off by poverty, distress and hunger was now robbed by her separation with her family. With time her smile faded and never returned thereafter as if she had suddenly grown out of her age.

She was treated well in Mr. Sharma's family. Now she took a bath with shampoo and soap, put coconut oil in her hair, wore a nice dress, was fed properly in return for doing the household works like cleaning utensils, washing clothes, cleaning the floors and even cooking food. Although her condition of living had improved in the new place, but, at night, when she retired for rest, she missed her family members, her mother, her younger brothers Pappu, Ladua and Chotka whom she carried in her arms, while her mother was at work. The thatched hut outside the village in which she and her family dwelt, was like the distant heaven for her. For some hours she would sob, weep and console herself before going to sleep.

Months passed, but Phulwa never smiled again, she resembled the lifeless flower plucked from a plant. Mrs. Sharma gave birth to a male child. When Phulwa took the new born baby in her arms, she remembered her youngest brother Chotka. After some days she fell sick. Mr. Sharma realized that the trauma of Phulwa's separation from her family had taken a toll on her. He decided to take her back to her village for a reunion with her family members. The news of her going back to her family served like a medicine and she recovered from her sickness, like some magical spell, cast on her.

When she boarded the train to go back, she became lively again. When she reached her house, she saw her younger brothers playing on the mud floor. She cried and ran towards her brothers. When her younger brothers saw her, they too ran towards her shouting and yelling "Phulwa didi", "Phulwa didi". All the four children hugged each other, laughing and crying, simultaneously, jumping, rolling on the dusty mud floor. Phulwa was soon filled with dust, her hair crisscrossed and locked all over her face. The poor children had reunited. Poverty and scarcity were acceptable to them, but, opulence, at the cost of separation was not. It was Phulwa's reunion with her smile and her family.

# Impaired Justice

Like many other hamlets, the tribal folk of Nijhar hamlet found a way out of their joblessness, when a coal mine became operational at Alubera; the villagers of Alubera were given the jobs as miners, diggers and loading and unloading workers. The villagers, whose villages or hamlets lay beside the road from the mining site to the coal dumping site, claimed their right over the coal by forcefully stopping the coal laden dumpers and taking five to ten kilogram of coal from every dumper that crossed their village road. The forceful collection from hundreds of dumpers accumulated into a huge amount of coal and every household of the village got a quintal of coal at an average daily. The condition for this illegal collection was that the villagers would vote for the party in power. The policemen would least bother about these illicit practices as they were gratified by the huge collection of bribes from those dumpers which were overloaded or forged the invoices.

The tribal folk of villages and hamlets like Nijhar, which were remotely situated, far from the main road, found their livelihood by risking their lives by illegally mining coal and collecting them in sacks. The sacks with approximately a quintal of coal would then be adjusted inside and over the triangular frame of the bicycle and the bicycle would then be pushed by them on foot and in this way they would cover some twenty to twenty five miles of journey on foot, pushing the coal laden bicycle from the mining site to its potential buyers in the town. The whole activity right from mining to carrying and selling took about two days of hard work and would fetch them eight hundred to thousand rupees, depending upon the bargaining potential of the buyers and sellers. Things would turn worse when some local media would be enraged when they would not get their share in this entire monkey sharing and they would either print or air the news of the loss being made to the state government's exchequer due to heist of coal. The police men would then be left with no other option but to capture some coal laden bicycles involved in the illegal trafficking of coal and go for a photo shoot in the police station, proving their innocence. The rest of the illicit activities would continue as usual, as disturbing the ecosystem of larger players would be like touching the hive of a swarm of bees, and it would be difficult to brush things under the carpet.

Churki Paharin had accumulated two thousand rupees by selling the Indian Dammar tree leaves, which were used for making leaf plates. In spite of her husband Munda Paharia, being an unemployed tribal youth addicted to drinking toddy in his never ending leisure time, her love for him made her believe that her husband would give up excessive drinking of toddy if he would get some employment. With much frugality she had managed to burgeon two thousand rupees.

On her marriage anniversary she took her husband to the Majhi-sthan, the place of worship of their tribal god. The tribal folk said their prayers completed their rituals and went to the town to buy a bicycle. The next day Munda got up early in the morning like a good husband got ready and hugged his wife before departing to start his new vocation like some of his fellow tribesmen, to mine coal, carry it on bicycle and sell it in the market. On his way he bowed his head at the Majhi-sthan, recited some prayers and headed for his new occupation.

With great risk he entered the man made cave heading towards the rocks of coal, mined the coal with a chisel and hammer, filled his sack with coal, adjusted one coal laden sack in the triangular frame of his bicycle and another sac above it and started his twenty five miles journey dragging his bicycle. While dragging his coal laden bicycle his black coloured skin glittered with drops of sweat accumulating on his skin and then falling on the ground which were replaced by more sweat on his skin. The veins and arteries protruded out of his lean and thin body, with his heart pumping blood at its optimum capacity. The scorching sun rays did not deter his craving to earn money by selling coal.

Fortune favours the brave but not the poor. As soon as he entered the town dragging his bicycle, he saw some policemen confiscating the coal laden bicycle, some yards before him. To save his hard earned bushel, he immediately took a left turn inside a narrow lane dragging his bicycle with full speed panting and gasping for air. The lane had many twists and turns like his fate. Bang! He collided with a tricycle on a blind turn and it triggered his brawl with the tricycle puller. Munda speculated his detrimental position, so he tried to end the wrangle by paying fifty rupees to the tricycle puller as a compensation for the broken spoke of his front wheel, but his opponent was in no mood to spare him for such a meagre amount and claimed two hundred rupees as compensation. Fifty rupees was all that Munda had for his lunch expenses. The loud tumultuous noise attracted the attention of a policeman who considered it his sacred duty, not to leave an opportunity of earning money. What mattered to him were the ends and not the means of earning money.

He heard both the parties, blamed both the opponents and settled the dispute by ordering the tricycle puller to manage his losses all by himself. Now he turned towards Munda who had almost surrendered his fate to the man in uniform. With a serious semblance on his face, he said that, as per law, his bicycle would be confiscated, along with the coal. Munda fell on his feet "Saheb, Saheb". This was the only vocabulary with which he could interact with the non-tribal. With a generous garb on his face the policeman said, "Ok dump this coal in my house, and catch your ears that you will never get indulged in theft of coal anymore."

Munda immediately rushed to the policeman's nearby house, dumped the coal, for free of cost and cycled back to his village. He drank a toddy of fifty rupees and forgot his miserable past. All his tiredness was absorbed by the intoxicated drink and he fell near the narrow pathway of his village.

At night, Churki came looking for him, splashed water on his face and helped him walk back to the hut, holding the bicycle with one hand and her husband Munda with the other hand. The tribal folk had no grudge, with what life had offered to them.

# Tribal Vanity

Hathigarh village witnessed a sanguinary fracas of two tribes, the Kisku and the Tudu, which left thirteen dead and nineteen wounded. The extrapolation being the dispute over possession of land for a decade and the spark being the harvesting of crops by the Tudu, which had been sown and taken care of by the Kiskus. The people of the vicinity could hardly believe the news of the deadly skirmish, by the tribal who would otherwise seem to be very circumspect and placid by temperament. The wee hours of Hathigarh village broke its silence, with a physical tussle between a couple of the Kisku tribal women, who protested against the male member of the Tudu tribe who had come to harvest the crop, which he believed was grown on his property. The squabble turned hellacious when a lady of the Kisku family cut open the throat of Santosh Tudu when she was pushed by him. Soon, the kins of both the families clashed with each other raining arrows at each other and the women of both the clans attacked their opponents with sickles. The battle was quick but indecisive as it all ended abruptly within an hour and ended with all the members of both the tribal clans either being dead or critically injured. The police as usual, arrived when it ended all by itself, only to carry on the formalities of sending the corpse for post-mortem and those injured to be hospitalized and collecting details of the First Information Report to be filed by them.

Maloti Kisku had fallen in love with Pradhan Tudu when they were high school students. Their attraction with each other led to their marriage by tribal rituals and soon led to the divorce with their academics. The young tribal folk were leading a happy and contented life by cultivating half of the twenty acres of Pradhan's ancestral property, and the other half was under the possession of his elder brother Santosh Tudu.

Maloti gave birth to a girl child Meeru who became fatherless before her first birthday, as Pradhan died in an accident. The death of Pradhan was a jolt in Maloti's happy life. But for Santosh it was a mixed compassion. He was sad and mourning his brother's death and at the same time felt felicitous that now he would have his claim over Pradhan's ten acres of land. According to tribal law a daughter could not claim her father's property. As Maloti did not have a son with Pradhan, as per the tribal law, she had lost the claim over the land that belonged to Pradhan, But according to the Indian constitution she had a legal right over her deceased husband's property.

It is human nature that they believe and want others as well, to believe in the law that suits them the best. In this case the tribal law was in Santosh's favour and the Indian constitution's law was in Maloti's favour. The matter reached the court of law and the lawyers of both the parties convinced them that the case would be won by them. The dispute was argued upon in the court of law for about a decade. In India Justice is not denied but it is delayed to an extent that it is at par with denial. The decade-long rivalry led to a vicious animosity between the Tudu and the Kisku families and slowly and steadily between the villages of the Tudus and the Kiskus.

In this world, loving someone is considered a vice but inheriting the feeling of hatred and animosity is deemed to be a virtue. The tribal folk who live in the vicinity of nature, inherit the merits of being peaceful, calm and live in harmony with each other and even with other clans but when it comes to the tribal pride, they can go to any extent for their tribal vanity. Even losses in the form of men and material are justified in the garb of sacrifice.

The strife left Meeru with a serious injury in her left leg which had to be imputed and to make the matter even more worse she was now an orphan. Luckily, there was no one on the Tudu side who could confront her for claiming control over her ancestral property.

She tried to cultivate the land, but as soon as she reached the plot the thought of the past violence traumatised her. She returned to her hut, tried to forget her violent past but to no use. The whole night, she kept on staring towards the sky thinking over the ways, to find peace of mind. She knew that there were many more orphans like her who might be having sleepless nights like her who were her kin but filled with animosity and vengeance.

Good sense prevailed upon her and she realised that hatred and vengeance in the name of tribal pride were nothing more than destruction that was the cause of their peril. The next day she went to the village headman and donated her land for the village football ground. The red colour soil of the football ground still witnessed rivalries but of a different kind, it was a rivalry to win the game of football between the two teams which comprised of the team mates belonging to different clans the Tudus, the Kiskus, the Marandis, the Hansdaks and many more. The excitement of the game had brought the clans together and they all had realised that the glory of their tribal vanity lay in living in harmony with each other.

# Vermilion Application Hymn via Satellite

Bablu Pandit was quite popular among the denizens of Kurapara, a locality where the people belonging to the lower middle class and lower class dwelt. Most of them were either less educated or illiterate. The reason for Bablu's popularity as a priest was not because he was a great scholar, but because his charges for carrying out religious prayers and rituals were quite less in comparison to his counterparts. He was a nice gentleman till his better half was alive, but after her death, he became a drunkard. The ancestral occupation was his source of meagre income, with which he took care of his three children, Shibu, Paro and Dinesh, and spent half of it as expenditure for his drinks. He had inherited the dexterousness from his parents and was excellent in the art of manipulation coupled with survival instincts, both of which were essential in the trade that he practiced, because he was not a scholar in the trade, which he pursued. He had learnt the hymns while he assisted his father in the ancestral occupation, but lacked flawlessness especially while chanting hymns with glutinous pronunciations.

In spite of being flawed in his vocation he would dexterously conceal his ineffectuality in chanting hymns by replacing the difficult pronunciation of some Sanskrit words by a vocal musical tone, which would portray him as a priest with high intellect in his vocation. His artifice could be apprehended only, by the people of his own profession, most of whom were travelling on the same boat, or by those who were well versed in Sanskrit Literature.

His day somehow passed being busy in his profession or gossiping with the people, but with the fall of night he would miss his wife and would not return to his house, as he knew quite well that, there was nobody, who would be waiting for his return, back home. His children were being fed and taken care of by his sister in law. The grief of his separation with his wife would direct him towards the toddy sellers near the pond. The intoxication of toddy would get him rid of the grief of separation with his wife and with a changed epithet, he would return home speaking a blend of English and Hindi languages and at the top of his voice, the meaning of which could only be understood by him and perhaps his deceased wife.

One day he was requested by a lower middle class Mandal family to perform the marriage ceremony of his daughter. The offer was immediately grabbed by Bablu Pandit as the money offered in return for carrying out the rituals of marriage would be a hefty amount. The marriage ceremony is a very long series of several rituals that are to be performed one after the other with continuous recitation of hymns in Sanskrit, which has immense power of developing a bond between the bride and the bridegroom who are expected to live or rather, tolerate each other for seven continuous births and rebirths.

The groom's wedding procession reached the bride's house late at night. Most of the guests from the bride's side had left for their homes after dining and could not be a witness to the wedding procession and the garlanding ceremony of the bride and the bridegroom. This angered the bride's relatives. The fire of anguish was fuelled by some of the relatives, who did not wish the marriage ceremony to go on smoothly. The untoward incidents of brawl in a marriage are like the pickles in a food plate, which add a unique taste to it, by activating the taste buds of the tongue. The antagonistic relatives find the marriage ceremony quite dull and monotonous in the absence of such brawls between the families of the bride and the bridegroom.

The late arrival of the groom's wedding procession gave such antagonistic relatives from both sides a golden chance which was utilized by them quite efficiently. The bride's father was foolish enough to fall into the trap and refused to give the golden chain to the bridegroom, as promised by him to the bridegroom's father, which waged a full scale war between the bride and the bridegroom's sides.

Every war ends up on the negotiation table, but the parties involved in a war reach the negotiation table only when both the parties are content with the specific objective being attained, by the heavy damage being inflicted to the enemy and to themselves. Vehemence ceases only after destruction.

The wrangle ended up with several relatives being injured from both sides and the fathers of both the bride and the bridegroom landing up in the police station. The police station In Charge initiated the negotiations and both the parties reached a truce.

The terms of cease fire were quite simple, the bride's father would hand over the golden chain to the bridegroom's father as he had promised, and the bridegroom's father would hand over the golden chain to the police station In Charge in return for the prisoners of war who were his relatives locked up in the police station. The cases of brawl and dowry would be overlooked by the Police, as it would ruin the bride's life, if the marriage would not be performed.

One can imagine the power of the hymns chanted during the marriage rituals and the divine power of the priest, which they derive from the affinity with God, that has the capability of reuniting the hostile clans into a matrimonial alliance that lasts for seven births and rebirths.

Frightened by the turn of events, the Pandit caught hold of the lower part of his dhoti, so that it would not obstruct his running away ceremony from the wrangle site. He took his refuge in the thatched hut of the toddy seller and doubled his routine quota of toddy in frustration and returned back to his house, as usual, with a changed personality, and fell asleep.

In the meantime, the two parties had signed a truce in the police station. It was two o'clock at night when they returned back for the marriage ceremony to take place. They found an important ingredient, the Pandit missing from the site. In the late night no other Pandit could be found and no other Pandit would dare to replace Bablu Pandit, as his clan was like a bee-hive, any action, which would hurt their ego, would invite the trouble of scores of his kin's wrath, buzzing and stinging like bees.

The bride's relatives went hunting for Bablu Pandit and reached his house. By this time, half of the influence of the intoxication of toddy was gone but the intensity of sleep was at its peak. Somehow, he opened the door of his room which opened to the roadside. As soon as he appeared at the door, the bride's relatives requested him to complete the rituals of the marriage ceremony. Bablu Pandit was in no mood to go with them, nor did the toddy that was still flowing through his veins permit him to do so. With a serious note and utmost divinity on his face he said, "Look, I've been chanting the hymns of the rituals throughout the time, you all were engaged in the brawl. It is the divine power of the mantras due to which a truce could be reached between the two hostile families. Since, I've been tired of chanting the hymns continuously, moreover I have chanted all the hymns that are necessary, you all do a very simple and easy task, go to the marriage mandapam, ignite the fire to the pieces of wood, that are kept there and exactly after twenty minutes, tell the bride and the bridegroom to revolve around the pious fire, seven times and the after that, the groom will apply vermilion on the bride's forehead to conclude the marriage. I shall be chanting the hymns from here and sending the positive vibes of the hymns of the vermilion application ritual via satellite".

# Informal Success

The State Board Exam's results had come with promiscuous reaction from the students, guardians, Education Department, and media. Some days back the matriculation results were declared with a whooping success rate of ninety four percent students passing their exams, the credit for which could be attributed to the large heartedness of the evaluators. All those who knew how to write and filled the papers with whatever literature they knew, had passed the exams. The evaluators of the higher secondary weren't smart enough to feel the nerves of what pleased the examinees, their guardians, the department, the Government and the print and the visual media, could fetch seventy percent of students passed, in the Arts stream and the Science stream's performance was below par with a meagre forty six percentage of students who had passed.

It led to a routine hue and cry and the blame game on teachers being paid a hefty amount of salary and underperforming. Accordingly, scores of punishments were slapped upon the teachers and in each and every meeting the teachers were reminded of the high amount of salary they received, as if cupboards stockpiled with high denomination currencies were unearthed by the Enforcement Directorates from the houses of the teachers. In fact their money income had been rising over the years but their real income, in terms of purchasing power had gradually deteriorated over the years, being almost half of what it had been twenty years back.

The teachers were dared not to speak a single word regarding the paucity of manpower and their engagement in election duties, census, and of course the marathon reporting on a daily basis, which left them with dwarfish time being left for their actual work, that was imparting education.

Nobody has the survival instincts more than that of the teachers. They learnt from their mistakes and the next year there was a miracle with the Intermediate results also hovering around ninety percent success rate. Only those students who wanted to fail and had left the answer sheets empty with no scope of being rewarded with marks. Sonamuni Hansdak was one among those unlucky, incapable students who couldn't pass the exams. In fact it was the second continuous year in which she couldn't pass the exam. Both Sonamuni and the educational system had failed each other.

Sonamuni's grandfather had been the owner of twenty five acres of land on the hill slopes of Palashbona village. He had been tricked by a fellow tribal and a Diku (non-tribal), both of whom were influential, capitalists cum politicians. They made him drink alcohol and had taken his thumb impression on the lease agreement papers. His protests were silenced by a small amount of money and alcohol as gifts. One day he died after consuming alcohol. Sonamuni's father had no other option but to start working as a laborer in the stone mine functioning on his own land. It was a common practice among the tribal, because they were innocent enough to be lured to lease away their land to the stone mining companies for meagre sum of money, and when the money they received were spent, they would work in the mines operating on their own land as labourers. They are the perfect examples of living in dearth amidst plenitude.

Success and failure are a state of mind. Sonamuni never took failure seriously. She knew that she had to work even harder to complete her studies, because her father could hardly support her with his low income coupled with the routine habit of drinking country alcohol. Sonamuni would get up early in the morning, cut grass from the hill slopes, make bundles of it, and sell it for ten rupees a bundle. Ten bundles of grass would fetch her hundred rupees, out of which she would use eighty rupees for her routine expenses and the rest twenty rupees would be saved by her for her studies. She realised that her absenteeism from regular classes was the reason for her failure in exams, so she decided to attend regular classes. She would skip her breakfast as the expense on breakfast would leave her with no money, to spare for the rent of the shared auto rickshaw with which she would go to the school that was seven miles away from her village. For some days she continued the practice but the system again failed her as three of the teachers appointed in the school could hardly spare their time for her subjects, because they were appointed for teaching different subjects. She understood that success without the help of a teacher would be improbable, so she approached one of the kind hearted teachers and requested him to guide her to pass her exams. The teacher gave his consent but in a few days he realised that Sonamuni had a language barrier, she could neither read nor write Hindi properly, forget about English. It was because of her incapability to write or read in Hindi properly that she could hardly memorize her lessons, or even write them. The questions in the Board Exams were bilingual, that is, in Hindi and English, and both the languages were alien to her. She knew Santali language, which was her mother tongue. The teacher realised that it would be quite difficult for Sonamuni to pass the exams with all these odds. He called her and asked why she wanted to pass the exam or carry on her studies, to which she immediately replied, "To get a job and earn money." The teacher answered with a smile, "If the purpose of studying is to earn money, then why are you running after these certificates, which are nothing more than papers? If they don't get you a job, don't waste your time and resources on these papers. Earning money is not a slave to these papers; there are millions of people who are quite well off, leading a luxurious life even though they are less educated in terms of certificates. This faulty education system has the wrong barometer to measure success. Ask yourself, what you are good at, sharpen the skill in which you are good at and deploy all your energy towards it, what may be called as an informal education."

Sonamuni went back home, thinking over each and every word that her teacher had told her, she had a sleepless night, the darkness of the night illuminated a new ray of hope in her that she could succeed, even without formal education. For some days she kept on thinking and one day an idea clicked in her mind, while she was selling grass to a middleman, who was engaged in buying and selling of goats, and lived a lavish life. She watched all his activities keenly, he would buy goats from the tribal folk as soon as they would approach the market place, tell them to collect money from him in the afternoon and in the meantime he would feed the goats, properly clean and oil them and sell it to the customers at a higher price and earned a hefty profit. He was smart enough to learn the Santali language to interact with the villagers. He was so smart in his vocation that he could even sell old and aged goats for a good price. He would purchase old goats with a broken tooth, and while selling the goat when the customer would try to investigate the wellness of the goat, he would smartly place his finger in the tooth gap of the goat and open its mouth with both the hands, and the customers could hardly find out the broken tooth of the goat.

Sonamuni had found the key to her success. For the next few months she collected money and with the proceeds bought a pair of goats, got them crossed with a he-goat and, within a year before the State Board results could declare some students as failed, she was the owner of a small herd of goats. She worked hard, in the morning she collected grass, not for sale in the market but for her goats. She reared goats and never sold to the middleman, but directly to the customers and made huge profits. Before her classmates could get a job of some thousand rupees, with their prized certificates, she was now earning lakhs of rupees per month.

One day she went to her teacher with a goat to give him as a present and thank him for his advice that had changed the course of her life. She touched the feet of the teacher and with a confidence on her face said, "Sir, my life has completely changed because of your advice, there is a question in my mind that can be answered only by you. Sir, why is the Government spending so much money after formal education, which is of least value when it comes to its practical use in earning money as means for survival? Why are we forced to waste our time and energy to learn the subjects two thirds of which are of no use to us in our practical life for our survival? Why do we have a faulty curriculum? The teacher replied with a smile, "Because the curriculum is not framed at the grass root level according to the needs and requirements of the beneficiary, but in the air-conditioned rooms in a far off distant place, by those whose feet rarely touch the ground."

# About the Author

Dr. Manish Gupta, has earned his Doctorate Degree in Economics. He is a gold medallist in Economics, with an experience in Academics of more than twenty three years. He is currently serving as the Principal of Chief Minister School of Excellence Girls, Pakur, in Jharkhand state. He has written many articles on a variety of topics, which have been published in national and International Journals. His stories are based upon true life experiences, upon a variety of social evils, which are targeted with sarcasm and humour. Every story has the capability to shake your conscience and awaken it. The ending of each and every story leaves you stunned. A must read story book based upon true events and experiences.

**From the Author's Page:**

This book, 'Conscience Pricked', is dedicated to My Mother who struggled hard to educate me against all odds. I further thank my teachers, friends and relatives who have been very kind, supportive and a source of inspiration for me. Last but not the least, I am indebted to my friend Neeraj Kumar, who had been very supportive in my school days.

This book 'Conscience Pricked' is a collection of ten stories based upon true incidents of life. Each and every story has a message to send to its readers, over a variety of social evils, which are targeted upon by means of sarcasm with a blend of humour. The stories will touch your heart, especially the concluding part. Such stories can be written by the one who has lived, experienced and struggled amidst poverty.